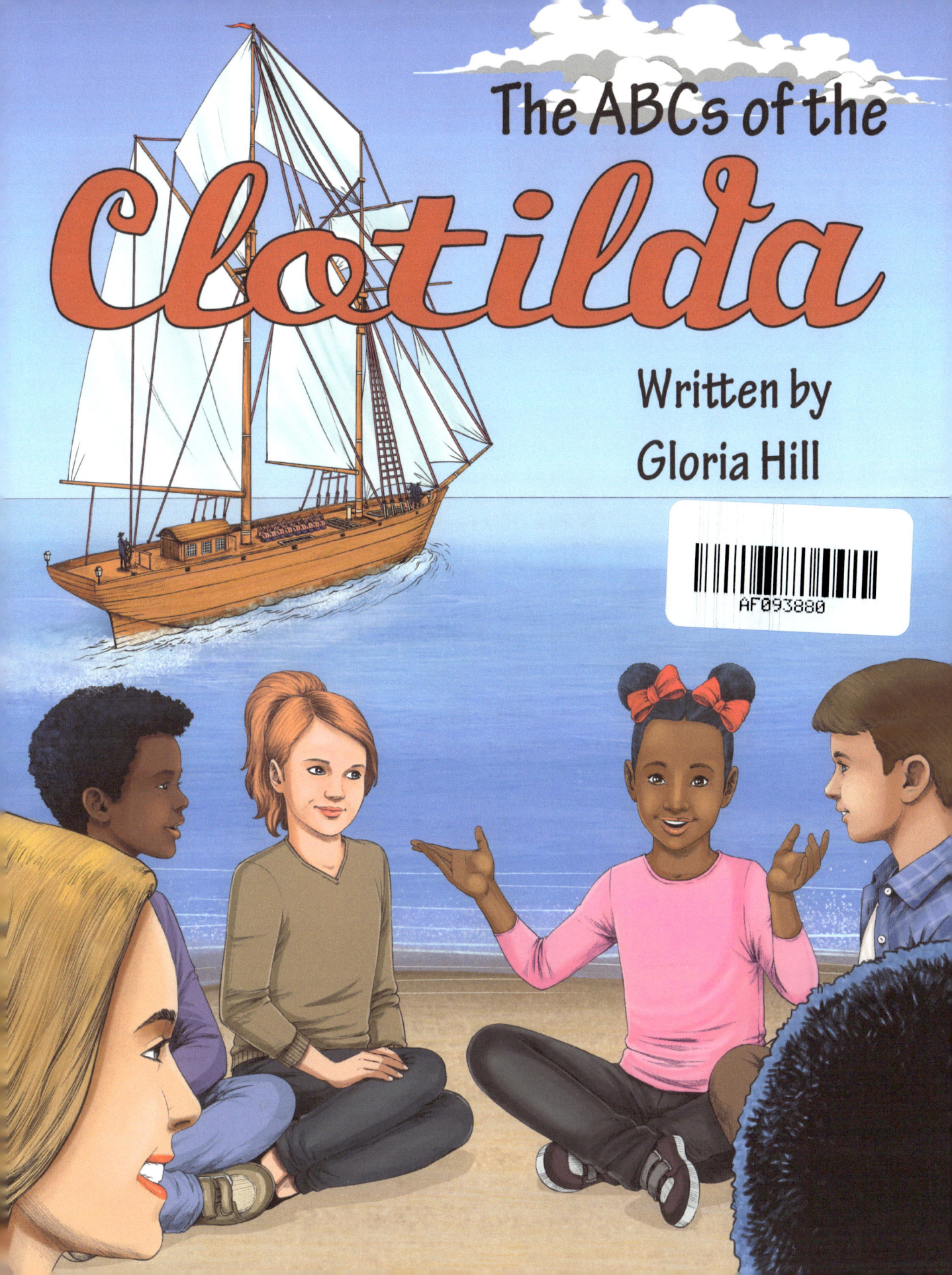

To my Granddaughter, Harriet

Proud, curious, self-assertive
Giving it all to the King
She's God's perfect little descendant,
Always standing in the gap for her people
A guiding light for descendants and descendants of descendants
Acknowledging the legacy for generations to come

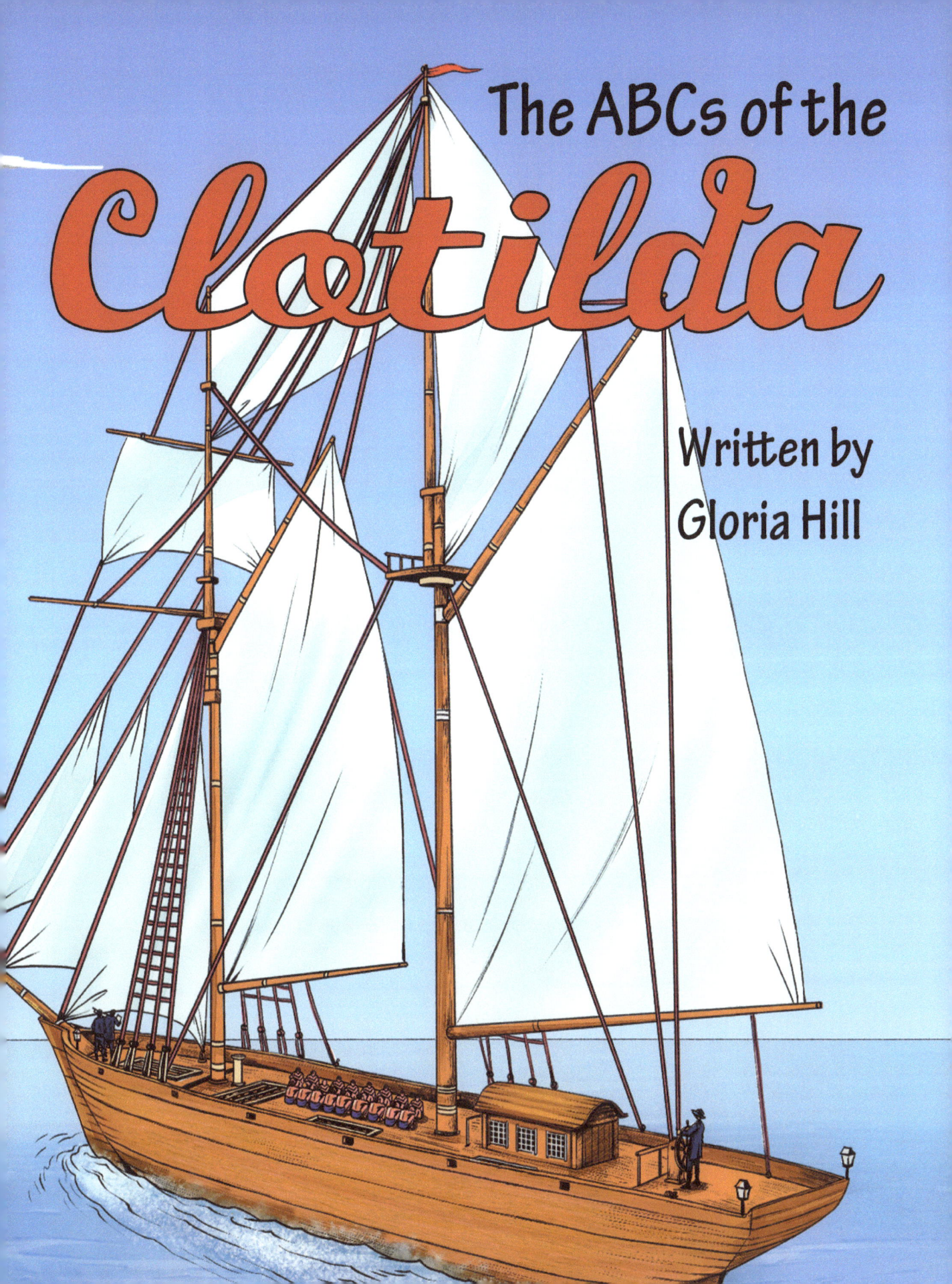

Acknowledgements

To two of the most curious admirers of
the Clotilda ever known:
Harriet and her father, Kel

Harriet is a bright and adventurous 5-year-old girl.
She lives in Mobile and attends Catholic School.
She loves to talk to her family and friends about the
captives who arrived at Mobile Bay in 1860 from
Africa on the last known U.S. slave ship, the Clotilda.

This book demonstrates the respect and profound love and admiration
for the legacy that my grandmother and I embrace in honor of our beloved
ancestors who boarded the Clotilda in Africa.

Confined with chains on a large boat, slaves were
ordered to leave the continent of Africa
and cross expanses of land to
the Southern United States.

The Clotilda is the last known slave ship.

Lame and impaired, slaves were ordered by slave masters to leave Africa to begin a new life in Southern America.

Oppressed and distressed slaves were forced to obey their slave masters and leave their country by slave ships.

Trapped and tangled, the slaves board the Clotilda, the last known slave ship, carrying 110 men, women, and children. It traveled from the western coast of Africa to Plateau, Alabama. The journey took 45 days.

Illegal slave trade isolated the slave families. With no choices, the slaves had to accept the inevitable that some of them would become ill.

Landmarks designate the boundary of where
the Clotilda docked in Africa Town
in Plateau, Alabama.

Descendants of the Clotilda helped establish the first Black high school, called Mobile County Training School.

Aftereffects of a significant unpleasant event
are evermore with the slaves forever.
We are each other's people.
We share each other's pain together.
We stand strong together.

Also by Gloria Hill

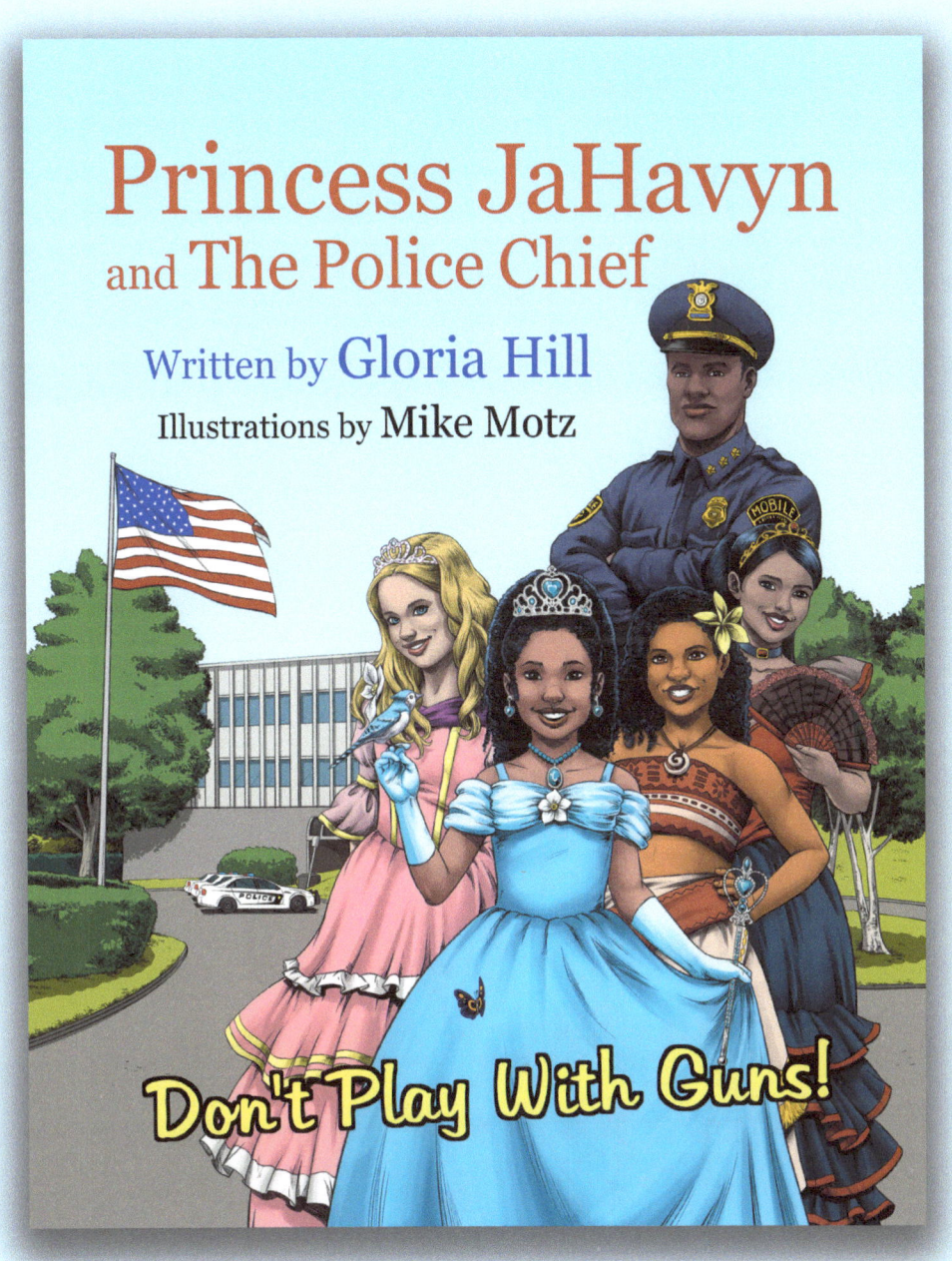

www.ingramcontent.com/pod-product-compliance
Lightning Source LLC
LaVergne TN
LVHW070443070526
838199LV00036B/690